Dancing Shadows in the LIGHT

Living with Chronic Illness;
Healing through Rhyme

KIMBERLY M. KLEIN

GENERAL INFORMATION

Dancing Shadows in the Light
Kimberly M. Klein

1st Edition: 2016

For information contact:
http://www.crystalvibrations.net

ISBN-13: 978-1523282692
ISBN-10: 152328269X

CREDITS

Author
Kimberly M. Klein

Editor
Subu "Sid" Shankar

Foreword
Andrew Williams, Ph.D.

Cover Graphics & Design
Kimberly M. Klein & Sarco Press

Illustrations by
Gus Mauk

(Deliver Me, Zombie Land, Rebirth, Light Worker, False Identities, Soul
Mate, Carpet Ride, Guardian Angel, Wolf Spirit, Dragon Guide, Keeping On,
Remembrance, Dancing Shadows)

Illustrations by
Gus Mauk & Lynzi Smith

(Simple Pleasures)

Illustrations by
Marco Roi

(Groundhog's Day #1, Spider's Tapestry)

Dedication ✍❤

This book can really only be dedicated to one person --my mother; the one who's been there for me through it all...the thick and the thin, the highs and the lows, the trials, heartaches and the tears.

I love you, Mom!

Table of Contents

GENERAL INFORMATION ii
CREDITS iii
Dedication ✍ v

Introduction *1*

Acknowledgements ✍ 3
Foreword ✍ 5
Preface ✍ 7

The Poetry *13*

Haywire ⤳ 15
Daily Grind ⤳ 16
F-Bombs ⤳ 17
Deliver Me ⤳ 19
Simple Tasks ⤳ 21
Just Be ⤳ 22
Frozen ⤳ 23
Zombie Land ⤳ 25
Misunderstood ⤳ 27
Cursed ⤳ 28
Metamorphosis ⤳ 29
Rebirth ⤳ 31
Let Go ⤳ 33
Surrender ⤳ 34
Healing Waves ⤳ 35

Light Worker ~ 37

Beautiful Day ~ 39

False Identities ~ 41

Poker ~ 43

Omens ~ 44

The Bard's Message ~ 45

Spider's Tapestry ~ 47

Imprisonment ~ 49

Resignation ~ 50

Acceptance ~ 51

Soul Mate ~ 53

Spoons ~ 55

Groundhog's Day #1 ~ 59

Thingy-Doo ~ 61

Left Behind ~ 62

Dusty Dreams ~ 63

Carpet Ride ~ 65

The Web ~ 67

Spring's Debut ~ 68

Mr. Finch ~ 69

Guardian Angel ~ 71

Wisdom ~ 73

Fear ~ 74

The Cave ~ 75

Wolf Spirit ~ 77

White Coats ~ 79

Constant Companions ~ 80

Guiding Light ~ 81

Dragon Guide ~ 83

Comrades ~ 85

The Calm ⁓ 86

Groundhog's Day #2 ⁓ 87

Keeping On ⁓ 89

Two Steps Back ⁓ 91

Simple Pleasures ⁓ 93

New Dawn ⁓ 95

Face the Sun ⁓ 96

Empowerment ⁓ 97

Remembrance ⁓ 99

The Shift ⁓ 100

Warrior of Light ⁓ 101

Dancing Shadows ⁓ 103

Epilogue *105*

About the Author ⁓ 107

Reviews ⁓ 109

x ～

Introduction

Acknowledgements ♥

I would like to thank my family and friends who believed in and supported me even when I didn't believe in myself.

Foreword ✍

The power of true art does not reside in the ornamentation or technical precision of the piece. It is not contained in the poetic flourishes of metaphor or the musical cadences of rhyme. The power of art; the power of poetry comes from the willingness of the poet to open a portion of her soul and let that bleed onto the page in so many words.

The poetry of Kimberly Klein is a brutally honest revelation of the crushing limitations of the body; a body that has betrayed its owner, but one that cannot suffocate the edifying spirit of the poet. Ms. Klein's poetry is about pain; it is about loss and the cruel intensity of losing control. But more importantly, her poetry is about the fortitude and strength of the individual spirit that refuses to succumb to the weight and whims of an uncaring fate. It is a testament to the power of her spirit to rise above that pain and allow her soul to bleed forth the lines that grace these pages.

The poems of Kimberly Klein are like windows into the powerful ordinary moments of an extraordinary life. We only have to take the time to gaze in.

Andrew Williams, Ph.D.
North Carolina Central University

Preface ✍♥

I have always been an introvert. The wallflower at social events and the school dance... the one, sitting alone in a corner amid a crowd of people. If you came up to me to start a conversation, I doubt it would go far, as engaging me in conversation is often futile. I would open my mouth to respond, but in so doing, a big fat nothing would spew from my lips.

My brain seems to be wired differently. I seem to have much difficulty with speaking my words yet they flow much easier when I am writing. For me, it's a connection from the heart to the hand.

Over the years, I tried numerous ways to write my story: inside a fictional, non-fictional, fantasy, humorous frame. Nothing meshed. I kept running into dead ends. One day, I made another attempt. Yet as the words still didn't seem to come, I was surprised to find a rhythmic tune humming in my mind instead... and along with the tune, the following words stumbled from my mind and fell onto the blank page before me.

> There's a book in my head
> Just waiting to get out.
> There's a book in my head
> Ready to shout.
> Ideas and images float easily through my mind,
> But putting words to the images
> Leaves me in a bind.
> My creative expression seems in a slumber.
> I'll be damned!
> My Muse has left me for another.

And then it hit me! "Why not tell my story in rhyme?"

My story began at the age of 18 when I was diagnosed with the debilitating disease of Multiple Sclerosis. Specialists offered me no hope. Unwilling to surrender to the crippling fate, I turned my hopes to alternative medicine. I learned numerous healing modalities over time, which helped keep the illness at bay for over 20 years. But then in my mid 40's, my health took a major nosedive. Tests revealed yet another autoimmune disorder more devastating than the first: Systemic Scleroderma. This illness left me utterly depleted... and housebound. I thought life stopped, only to realize that life never stops; it is always unfolding, always changing, like the rhythms of one season flowing into another.

Not being in the real world anymore, I turned within to look for answers and found a whole new world just waiting for me. In the solitude of silence, I discovered a wealth of information and friendships, all helping me on my journey of self-discovery and ultimately, self-healing. I was guided to turn my attention towards the Divine, the spiritual realm of angels, spirit guides, and guardians, as well as Nature and her animals. They are all forms in which Spirit speaks to us, offering messages of hope, guidance, and encouragement.

During that time, I learned that when life seems to offer us nothing but a series of challenges, we are being asked to look at the experience from a different perspective. When Spirit guides us to turn our focus inward, deep within our hearts, S/He is not only nudging us to find the lessons presented with each challenge, but to look and be thankful for the blessing within each challenge as well. By doing so, I was able to find my true self and allow Spirit to sustain me on my journey of self-healing and self-discovery. Writing has become a part of that journey, encouraging me to express and heal those deep emotions I struggle with on a daily basis-- to face the demons within, to share experiences of battles won and lost, of tears shed, and of finding the faith to continue on.

My intention with this book is twofold: To help empower others to overcome their own health challenges and difficulties by keeping an attitude of faith, knowing they are not alone in their experiences and to create more awareness, compassion and understanding among family, friends, and caretakers who deal with the dis-eased and dis-abled in their daily lives, as well as the world at large.

Kimberly Klein

"I will love the light
For it shows me the way.
Yet I will endure the darkness
For it shows me the stars."

~ Og Mandino

The Poetry

Haywire

Throughout the years,
My life has somehow gone awry.
The twinkling stars once suspended
Have now fallen from the skies.
My life seems nothing more
Than a night dark and bleak.
Some semblance of hope,
I wish to seek.

Daily Grind —

It's 1 PM and I'm still in my pajamas.
I can barely get away from the throne.
People keep calling, wanting to visit
But I just want to be left alone.
No one understands how my energy is sapped,
A smiling face I can no longer don.
The walking dead I have become,
The spark of life is now gone.

F-Bombs

I am frustrated beyond compare
As the F-bombs spew from my lips.
"Nothing is working!" I cry,
Not my hands or my legs nor my hips.

"How much more can I take?" I shout,
To the Creator up above,
The strong yet gentle voice responds, "My child,
You need only surround yourself with love."

"I know you think I have forsaken you,
But this I have not.
Trust, faith, belief in me...
Feel them with all of your heart."

"Soon you will realize I have always been here,
It is you who shut me out.
Be grateful for the blessings in your life
And never again wallow in doubt."

Deliver Me —∽

I no longer believe in going to Hell
For I live there each and every day.
Death, peace, and deliverance...
For these things, I pray.

The tears can no longer fall
Yet I whimper myself to sleep.
This cross I bear I can no longer endure,
Each night I beg for reprieve.

My organs and arteries are turning to stone,
My skin feels like taught leather.
My symptoms severely worsen with
The slightest change in weather.

Spring and Fall were once my favorite,
But now they are only seasons of pain.
Oh, how I wish I were free to enjoy
And fully live my life again!

Dancing Shadows In the Light

Simple Tasks

Many people take for granted
The simple tasks each day brings:
To clean the house, brush your teeth,
Or even cook Chinese,
To drive a car, walk in the grass,
To run and play with their pets in the park.
Yet all of these things evade me
As my body keeps falling apart.

Just Be —

I want to sit in the quiet
And be as still as still can be.
To listen to the flowers and the trees
Whisper their secrets to me.
A delightful chorus of chirping birds
In lovely harmony they sing.
To my heart, mind and soul,
Peace and happiness they bring.

Frozen

I wish to share a journey,
My life's story to tell
Of the challenges and trials,
Of living in Hell.

My hands have morphed into claws,
My body, like a petrified tree.
My, oh my!
What's happening to me?

Has my heart hardened so much
That I am now turning to stone?
I'm frozen in time, it seems,
And I feel so alone.

I cry out to the silence,
'Whatever am I to do?'
"Be gentle with yourself," Spirit replies
"And let My love move through you."

Zombie Land

I awaken in the morning
With my energy levels in the red
The day to follow
Can bring nothing but dread.
So many things
On my list of "To Do's"
Yet I've only the means
To accomplish one thing or two.
The fatigue is so crippling
And no one understands
That I can't even fathom
Menial demands.
What's that phrase,
They recently coined?
Oh, yes! It's the Zombie Apocalypse
And I have now officially joined.

Misunderstood

During this life,
Alone I've felt
Hiding away,
Never asking for help.

My demeanor judged
As aloof and smug,
Yet all I wanted was
Understanding and love.

Cursed —

Like most men in my life
They went running for the hills,
Once they found out about
My many chronic ills.

I always thought love
Was about for better or worse,
But my ill health became
Nothing but a lifetime curse.

Sad and heartbroken
I walked my path alone,
Without a true mate
To ever call my own.

Why couldn't they simply see
My radiant beauty within?
As everyone knows that with time
The physical attraction dims.

A valuable lesson in self-worth
Was greatly put to the test:
If a person can't love me at my worst,
They surely don't deserve me at my best.

Metamorphosis —

I feel myself changing
Said the Caterpillar to the Butterfly.
I see myself changing
But I don't know why.

I feel myself emerging
Said the Cocoon to the Butterfly.
I see myself emerging
But I don't know why.

"A beautiful creature," said the Butterfly
"Like me you soon will be
With wondrous, new wings
To fly for all eternity."

Rebirth —

Past lives come and past lives go
With each life experience
We slowly, but surely grow.

Enduring strife, struggle and pain
All the while aspiring to find
Our true being once again.

But 'baptism by fire' I chose this time around.
The phoenix now rising from the ashes
That had once been burned to the ground.

From the ashes, the Phoenix will rise.
From the ashes, the Phoenix takes flight.
Its magical essence, renewed and restored.
A spiritual alchemist has now been reborn.

Let Go ⤳

What is surrender?
Many ask but do not hear
The wondrous answer
Whispered in their ear.

Many years it took
For me to understand
The simplicity of surrender,
That makes miracles expand.

Letting go, and letting God
Is what it is all about.
Let Him do the heavy work
With this, I have no doubt.

Surrender

Lord, please cure me
From head down to my toes!
When this will happen,
Nobody knows.

Hold me in your
Loving embrace.
Let your healing energy
Flow from grace.

"Faith and trust are
The means to an end.
Belief in Me will
Help you wholly mend."

Healing Waves

I can listen to the ocean's waves
For hours at a time,
Washing away the worries I have
And the limiting beliefs that bind.
Dissolving all negative debris
Making me crystalline pure,
An empty vessel I've become
Now able to heal from my core.

Light Worker —

I have finally come home to my place by the sea,
A warrior princess I will always be.

A keeper of the Earth
And all she holds dear,
The sacredness of all that is,
To my heart I hold near.
All beings of the Universe
Live in harmony as one,
For this I will fight
Until it is done.

A peaceful world finally prevails
Where all is made aright,
The dawning of a new, Golden Era
Streams forth with Love and Light.

Beautiful Day ~

Oh, what a beautiful morning!
Oh, what a beautiful day!
I can't wait to get out of bed
And go outside to play.

I turn over to greet the Sun
His rays shining brightly in my face,
I beam a smile back at him
But feel something's out of place.

The sleepiness washes away
As I now fully open my eyes.
Reality edges its way in
And all too soon I realize.

My day of wonder
Has now turned to dread,
As I look upon the leg braces and crutches
Securely tucked near my bed.

I try to grab my legs with crippled hands
That are barely able to grasp.
The feats of my day have just begun
With this very first task.

I return my look to the window
And that big ball of fire in the sky,
As tears stream down my face
Falling gently from my eyes.

For me, playtime is but a fantasy
Only battles lay ahead.
Into the dreamtime I wish to retreat
And upon a pillow, lay my weary head.

False Identities —⌒

I live my life vicariously through
The characters in my books
As I sit quietly and contently
In my cozy, little nook.

One day, I'm a princess,
The next day, I'm a wicked queen.
Or even a blood-sucking vampire
That makes me want to scream.

A warrior in the Highlands,
A kid at summer camp
At times a Romanian gypsy
Or an alluring tramp.

A rider of dragons
And a sorcerer, too
Who conjures spells
From out of the blue.

My days are filled
With magic and wonder
As I excitedly await
The lifetime of another.

Poker

Life is never easy
No matter how it's sliced or diced.
While some are blessed with smooth journeys,
Others are carved from ice.
It is what it is!
It's time to let it go.
Either play the hand you have been dealt
Or give up and fold.

Omens

I am surrounded by a myriad
Of spiritual guardians and guides,
A wealth of wisdom and awareness
They graciously provide.

Spirit speaks to us in many ways
Offering numerous clues,
Through angels and ascended masters
And a multitude of animal totems, too.

There are hidden forces of Nature
Woven into every aspect of our lives.
We merely need to become aware
Of their many sacred insights.

The Bard's Message

The Bard appeared in my life today
In all his fine glory,
Asking me to seek answers
In my life's personal story.

"Look at the threads and patterns
That are repeated throughout time,
Weaving the fabric of your being
And events of your life.
The seeds of your future
Are always hidden in the past.
Don't be afraid to look and learn,
Courageously take the chance.
Memories and messages
Will flow through your mind,
As the strings of your soul
Are strummed beautifully by the Divine."

Spider's Tapestry

I keep running towards you
Yet you keep running away.
The ignorance keeps you imprisoned
While my message gets delayed.

As Spider, I am a weaver of life's fate,
A symbol of the feminine divine.
I superbly spin my silky threads
Creating patterns through time.

Through your thoughts, feelings and actions
The design of your life unfolds,
Integrating all aspects of yourself
While making you whole.

I am often found in the darkness
Creating intricate designs at night.
My majestic tapestry remains hidden
Until it glistens at dawn's early light.

Imprisonment —◦

My freedoms are being taken away one by one,
A lowly prisoner I've become.
Doing time for the crimes of my past.
How long will this punishment last?

This karma thing really bites the dust!
But reaping seeds once sowed is always a must.
Weeks turn into months and months into years
The restrictions causing me nothing but fear.

But the prison is of my own making
And the limitations are self-imposed.
I will be here forever and a day
Until my false beliefs are transposed.

But the day of reckoning does finally come,
When the prison doors swing open
And freedom is sung.

As I cross the mighty threshold
The guards whisper in my ear:
"Some hard lessons you have learned
Yet you've successfully persevered.
Now you have the wisdom
And the secrets of your soul.
It's time to finally face the Light
And let your true Self unfold.

Resignation —⟋

A plethora of heinous symptoms
Has become a daily grind,
Even a thread of positive energy
My body lacks to find.
The fatigue itself is quite crippling to me
Both in body and mind,
The monster that ceaselessly drains my strength
Has been anything but kind.
So now, enclosed in my own house
I've been duly confined,
Living a life of mere existence
To this, I have fully resigned.

Acceptance ～⤴

Acceptance does not mean resignation
But to befriend and transform
The very enemy you are fighting
And trying to destroy.

Soul Mate

I love my familiar. Yes, I do!
Heart to heart and through and through.

I love the essence of her soul
She's made me happy...made me whole.

The sole survivor from a litter of eight
To the pound, the next day
This kitten they'd take.

Alone and scared,
She scampered across my path,
Laid on my feet, then clawed up my pants.

She nestled her way into the pocket
Of my hoodie made of fleece,
Where she slept for many hours
Finding comfort, contentment, and peace.

That night I found my soul mate
Or I guess, she actually found me.
With a purr and knowing nod, she mewled,
"Together we'll always be!"

Spoons

I can't take credit for the 'Spoon Theory,'
But thought I'd pass it along,
To help healthy people understand
And see what's going on.

A person enduring chronic illness
Is only given a certain amount of "spoons"
To think about and use wisely
To make them last 'til after noon.

Twelve spoons I've been blessed with today
To gauge and be methodically placed.
I must be very careful
So my spoons don't go to waste.

At the crack of dawn, the first one is used
To simply open my eyes.
The second to wrestle out of bed
"I'm already down to ten!" I cry.

The third is used for some bathroom duties
'Some' being the operative word.
After a tinkle in the pot and a brush of my teeth,
My shower is now deterred.

I head out of the bathroom
Dragging my legs down the hall,
Watchful of every step I take
Just so I don't stumble and fall.

Phew! I've barely made it to the kitchen
Where I need to sit and rest.
Only half an hour has passed
And another spoon was put to the test.

I'm quickly becoming frantic
As my day has just begun,
Four spoons I have wisely used
Yet it feels like Armageddon!

The battle wages on as I fight
To keep my spoons close at hand,
Yet the daily events keep adding up
And my spoons are now in high demand.

I've showered and dressed. Ugh!
Four more spoons have been repossessed.
To this request I was rather
Disinclined to acquiesce.

Only four spoons remain
To last through the rest of my day
"However should they be used?" I ask
To this, I can only kneel and pray.

But kneeling is out of the question
So sitting is what I do

For the remainder of the day, in fact
Just to make it through.

Spoon Theory –

The term spoons was coined by Christine Miserandino on her website, But You Don't Look Sick. In the article "The Spoon Theory" she recalled a conversation in which her close friend and roommate asked her a vague question about what having lupus feels like. As the two were in a diner, Miserandino spontaneously took spoons from nearby tables to use as a visual aid. She handed her friend the spoons and then asked her to describe the events of a typical day, taking a spoon away after each hypothetical activity. In this way, she demonstrated that spoons, or energy, must be rationed to avoid running out before the end of the day. Miserandino also asserted that it is possible to exceed one's daily limit, but that doing so means "borrowing" from the future, and may result in not having enough spoons the next day.[1]

Groundhog's Day #1 ⁓

I need a vacation from my body
For forever and a day.
I'm so friggin' tired
Of my life being like 'Groundhog's Day!'
How am I supposed to love my body
When all it does is cause me grief?
I watch it deteriorate daily
Without ever getting a reprieve.

Thingy-Doo

My mind has become discombobulated
As discombobulated as can be
Thinking and speaking simple words
Simply evade me!

What's that doohickey on the thingamajig?
Or that whatchamacallit over there?
I grasp for common words
But can't find them anywhere!

So when I say, "I like your thingydoo"
Please take no offense.
I'm merely giving you a compliment
As I've obviously lost all common sense!

Left Behind —

Even though I can't often go places,
It would still be nice to be asked.
Rarely being offered to be a part of things
Leaves me feeling a complete outcast.
I wonder how they would feel
If they were in my shoes?
I'm sure they'd be doing nothing
But singing the blues.

Dusty Dreams ~

It's not easy living
A life filled with chronic ills
I'd much rather be dirt old and over the hill.

At least then I could be grateful
For having lived my dreams.
Being sick and disabled leaves me
Feeling anything but peace.

I wish my dreams were memories
But they're merely fantasies,
Floating through my mind.
Like dust being scattered in the wind,
Those dreams I've now left far behind.

Carpet Ride

A beautiful Magic Carpet
My friend gifted me today.
"It's time to hop on," she said
"And let yourself play."

May it take you to far away places
And set your imagination free.
The possibilities are endless!
You soon will see.

You can be anywhere, anytime
In the blink of an eye.
Simply ride with the beauty
Found within your mind.

The Web ~

It's quite interesting to see
From birth to death
The web of life that we weave,
From words and deeds
And thoughts we think
To every breath we breathe.

Spring's Debut

I love sitting quietly on my sun porch
When the April rains make their seasonal debut,
Watching the trees bud and the flowers bloom
Creating Mother Earth anew.

Mr. Finch ⌒

Mr. Finch made an appearance today
Sporting his vibrant colors of black and gold.
What message could he possibly have for me?
I surely wanted to know.

"A close connection to Mother Nature, you have,
And a deep understanding of her ways.
You live on the edge of the Spirit world
To this, the Animals and Faeries sing praise.
But it's time to come out of the shadows,
And step into your own Light.
The Ascended Masters are with you
When the Gold Finch takes flight.
You are being reminded to live in the now
And to savor each and every minute
For life is for the living,
Embrace the joys within it."

Guardian Angel

I send you
This loving Angel
To be with you
Each and every day,
To guide and watch over you
Every step of the way.
To enfold you in his loving wings,
Guarding and protecting you
From all harmful things.
To light your path
On life's journey
And help free you from
All of your worries.

Wisdom

I try to stay positive
Through my trials and tears,
Yet my health continues to worsen
Over the months and years.

Discouraged and disheartened
My life proves nothing but bleak,
It is now sage advice
That I will need to seek.

"Drop into your heart," whispered Spirit
"You will find me there.
Spend time with Me in the silence
And all will be made clear.
I AM your greatest teacher,
Answering all that you ask.
It doesn't matter your query
Whether it's present, future, or past.
You worry about your illness
Yet your fear and illness are one and the same,
When you finally release the fear
Your illness will fade".

I have often looked to many others
To answer all that I have asked,
But found it's within my own Being
Where true wisdom is unmasked.

Fear —

You can't escape your demons,
That's a definite truth in life.
And you can't give in to the darkness,
You must take a stand and fight.

You are stronger than you remember.
You must show them who you are.
There is help and love all around you,
You don't need to look far.

Only you can choose how your life will unfold
And only you get to decide.
You must believe your fears aren't real,
If you truly want to survive.

The Cave

No one ever said
Life would be easy or fair,
So I've taken to living
In a cave with Bear.

The lessons I've learned
Are way beyond measure.
Time alone in my heart's sanctuary
Has been a golden treasure.

The true essence of my being
Was found by going within.
Living in the outer world,
It could never have been.

The song of my soul now sings
Nothing but praise.
Hallelujah! I decree,
For the rest of my days.

Wolf Spirit

The daytime sun
Brings laughter and a smile,
But with nighttime's darkness
Echoes the wolf's lonely howl.

The Spirit Wolf is my constant Guide
Traversing through spiritual tests,
Guiding me through dimensional gateways
To help me be my very best.

He helps me gather frayed ends of emotions
Along with the fragments of my soul,
Binding them back together
In order to make my being whole.

White Coats

How can I trust the white coats
When they offer nothing but dread?
Who gave them the right
Telling me when I'd be dead?

I could never forget being diagnosed
With a disabling illness in my teens:

"It's incurable," they said,
"And can't be healed by any means.
By the age of 21
In a wheelchair you will be,
Paralyzed forever
You will never be free.
And a probable untimely death
Before the age of 43."

The crushing analysis was given...
The hopeless path set before me.

My world was now cloaked in darkness
And my life had gone awry
As the sinister shadows had been cast
Over the lot of my life.

Constant Companions —

I can no longer stand myself
Nor put on a brave face,
Tired and weary I've become
Living in a dark place.

My heart and soul scream out for help
But even hope does not come.
Mentally speaking,
I've become quite undone.

Despair and despondency
Are now my constant friends.
A wonderful life...
I can no longer pretend.

Guiding Light —

I am here to guide you
And help you through the day,
To help you see the light
On your journey's way.

A steadfast lighthouse with my light
Shining brightly ever near the sea,
Illuminating your pathway
So you can easily find me.

Am I love? Am I wisdom?
Am I a treasure you hope to find?
Keep looking to the Light,
And leave all fears and worries behind!

Dragon Guide

As I search the heavenly stars
In the thick of the night,
I beckon to Dragon,
My guiding light.

Guardian and protector,
A lifetime friend
His gifts graciously given to me,
Of courage, fortitude, and strength.

Comrades —ᷣ

Metatron and Michael
Raphael and Gabe,
The Archangels are with me
Each and every day!

They offer guidance, love and support
They're there through thick n' thin
They light my path when darkness falls
And greet me when my day begins.

Without their omnipresence
Where would I be?
Quite lost and alone, I'm sure,
On my life's arduous journey.

The Calm —

The beach brings solace.
The beach brings peace.
It is here where my soul and I meet.

The ebb and flow of the ocean's waves
Create rhythm in my being
In so many ways.

My body starts to sway
To the beat of an internal hum.
My heart, mind and soul
Now dance in harmony as one.

Groundhog's Day #2

Will this ever end...
This suffering of mine?
All I do is sit here,
Making up rhymes.
I live in a small world
Created in my head.
Groundhog's Day
Never friggin' ends!

Keeping On —

The winds of change are upon me
It is time to release that which binds.
I am trying to keep ahead of my thoughts
And to not look behind.

It's not easy marching into uncharted waters
But I can't let fear keep me tied to the shore.
Every journey begins with one single step
And I know God's plan for me holds so much more.

It has been a long journey out of the darkness
But I am now well on my way.
The path continues to get brighter
With each and every passing day.

Two Steps Back

When we see no way of moving forward,
We often turn backwards instead.
It's more of going deep within
Where the lights and shadows live.
Dark times bring growth and healing
By shedding light upon our fears,
Helping us face adversity
And giving the strength to persevere.

Simple Pleasures —☙

I've learned to be grateful
For the simple pleasures in life,
To see the wondrous and majestic
Amid many years of strife.

I am thankful for the beauty
Found in every day,
And for unknown blessings
Already on their way.

I am thankful for the sun
That shines its warming rays,
For snow that magically glistens
And for nurturing rains.

I am thankful for the wind
That blows gently in my ear.
I am thankful for the birds and bees
That always bring me cheer.

I am thankful for the moon
That lights the evening sky,
And for twinkling stars
That softly blanket the night.

I am thankful for brilliant rainbows
Splaying their prismatic hues,
And for puffy white clouds
Suspended in skies of azure blue.

I am thankful for family and friends
That daily grace my life,

For the many lessons learned
And finding peace within my plight.

I am thankful for the angels and animals
And the Divine messages they bring.
But it is for my life, I am thankful for
More than anything.

New Dawn

I've endured many storms over rough seas
But the way has now been made
Smooth and clear.
I expect the best from here on out
And wash away all
Negativity and fear.

I let the weight of past memories
Fade gently away,
Keeping only the lessons learned
So the same drama isn't replayed.

By extracting the positive teachings
I've turned a new corner on my path,
Moving into a life of blessings and miracles
It's a New Dawn at last!

Face the Sun —☙

Turn your face to the Sun,
Let the shadows fall behind.
I promise that love and blessings
Will follow in kind.

Turn your face to the Sun,
And never look back!
Your world is wonderfully changing
From a lifetime of effort and lack.

Turn your face to the Sun,
Let the darkness fade to Light!
It's time to step into your greatness
Allowing your essence to shine bright.

Turn your face to the Sun,
Stand in the truth of who you are!
For the radiance of your soul
Is known among the stars.

Empowerment —◌

Skipping down the yellow brick road,
My ruby slippers I hoped to find,
When the Lion, the Scarecrow and the Tin Man
Approached me from behind.

The Lion taught me,
"It's courage in your soul you need to seek."

The Scarecrow told me,
"It's positive thoughts you need to think."

"But," said the Tin Man,
"It is in the heart where your
Empowerment reigns,
And with an open heart
Gratitude wins the game."

Remembrance

You are as magnificent as the sunrise
And as ancient as the stars.
It is time to wake up
And remember who you are.

May your light and kindness
Flow gently into the world.
May your presence grace the Earth
And your true radiance shine forth.

You are here to light the pathway
For all others to see,
And to help guide them on their journeys
For all of eternity.

The Shift —℠

My life's patterns and paradigms are shifting
As my body shudders in fear.
My blueprint's constructs are changing
As the divinity within now begins to reappear.

Warrior of Light

I am a woman of strength.
I bend. I do not break.
Yet my body bleeds...
And my heart aches.

I am a woman of strength.
I am blessed even in my darkest hour.
That is when the Creator moves through me,
Activating my spiritual power.

I am a woman of strength.
I was created to survive!
For I AM
A Warrior of the Light.

Dancing Shadows

Shadows dancing in the light,
Pick up your swords! It's time to fight.

A battle-hardened warrior I've become
Donning my suit of chinked armor.
Bruised and battered,
I tread the path of bloody sorrow.
Accursed with gnarly scars,
I've grown weary and alone.
A glimmer of Angels graces the horizon
Beckoning me to come home.

Many battles have been lost
Yet I continue to trudge on.
The war, a possible triumph
'Til the sounding of the swan's song.
The devil's labyrinth appears
A trick he often plays,
Presenting insurmountable feats
In a seemingly endless maze.

But of all the weapons taken into battle
The most important is the mind.
By vanquishing the demons within,
Victory is certainly mine!

Epilogue

About the Author ℰ⤸

The victory isn't the healing...it's living the day-to-day darkness of disease until the healing is manifested....

We often take our health for granted, as if it will always be here...until it's not. Author Kimberly Klein has never taken her health for granted and never will. Diagnosed at 18 with multiple sclerosis and in her 40's with systemic scleroderma, Ms. Klein learned a stark truth: surrender was not an option. She would thrive in spite of her circumstances!

Taking control of her health started with a courageous journey into the Self. Ms. Klein learned to shed the limiting beliefs shadowing her thoughts and released the emotional wounds that kept her stuck in self-defeating paradigms. Kimberly

Klein's mindset was only the first step to ultimate healing. The biggest challenge was twofold—the persistence of the illness and learning the disease itself was the path to healing the heart and the spirit. From there success followed success as negativity and fear melted away.

Bookstores are filled with self-help books and memoirs written by authors who battled serious illness and have healed themselves. They bask in their victories, grateful to have escaped the "dark night of the soul". What separates Ms. Klein from her contemporaries is the unique perspective of her writing. Her poignant prose and eloquent descriptions provide a vivid glimpse of the day-to-day struggle living in the shadows of disease. Her message is clear and strong— people must become aware of themselves and others. We must learn to be kinder, more compassionate and more understanding of those who do not lead a "normal" life. Love is the essence of healing. Overwhelming agape love.

A Reiki Master/Instructor, Holistic Counselor and Intuitive Energy Healer, Kimberly Klein resides in Pennsylvania's Laurel Highland Mountains where she practices various alternative therapies, teaches Reiki and Iridology, and helps to empower others on the path to wholeness. To learn more about Ms. Klein, please visit www.CrystalVibrations.net

Reviews ✐♥

'Dancing Shadows in the Light' is a truly compelling work of a poet working through her daily challenges with health and life. Kimberly Klein's epic struggles have formed the fertile playground for her creative expression. She manages to pull intense, poignant verse out of dark reality just as well as she scales mountaintops of inspiration with a tough but rewarding muse. Her journey is a metaphor for the path of the warrior soul, who resides in each of us. One easily relates to her verse without having to experience her debilitating condition; therein lays her skill as a poet—the transmutation of her pain into throbbing emotion and shining wisdom, which have the evocative power to fill any fellow warrior up. In this uniquely composed collection of poems, there is rich interplay of the threat of shadows and the healing power of light to the point where all that matters is the dance. The dance of creation.

~ **Subu 'Sid' Shankar**, Writer and Editor
Mumbai, India

—ᜃᜃ—

The reader of any book, I feel must be captivated and be able to identify with what we write! It is in the vulnerability of the writer, the openness of the heart and soul to communicate with us the reader. I have gone through so much pain and sorrow, both in my body, my heart and emotionally. I did not think anyone really could understand what I have gone through. You simply just cannot really explain it to people! Then I read Kimberly's

poetry and I was completely captivated by her raw expression, and her heart completely naked to me. As I read each poem for the first time, I knew someone else understood my pain and sorrow. As I read them again I felt a deeper freedom come to my own heart. I felt a relief that I was not crazy and I was not the only one to experience such in-depth pain and sorrow, then finding that deep connection to God and healing through it all. I commend her for her nakedness of the Raw expression of her heart and soul. I hope many will find deep healing through her willingness to put her heart and soul out there for others to see and experience!

~ **Aaron Pierson,** Author
Udon Thani, Thailand
www.spiritualhealing-enlightenment.us

—∭—

Reading Kimberley's poetry, for me has been a truly interesting and liberating experience, as this work of hers is so powerful , so beautiful, that it reached right into my heart and tugged at it. The power of the experiences she conveys through her poetry is so graphic, and then there is the beautiful spiritual essence of the poetry being threaded through the centre of it which makes it even more powerful. I have looked through them again to try and identify a favourite, but I cannot... for each one of these poems has its own special value. My spiritual belief system becomes fortified even further when I see the power of Kimberley's spirit shining through all that she has endured.

~ **Elizabeth Slingsby**, Reiki Master/Teacher/Owner
The Peaceful Planet Healing and Teaching Practice,
Preston, Lancashire, England
www.thepeacefulplanet.co.uk

—∭—

The honesty and passion of Ms. Klein is clear through this series of poems. As someone who is sensitive to energy, it's easy for me to get right into the feelings of the author, and although not the most light and airy content, it is clear that she writes as a form of self-healing, which is very important. I am rooting for Kimberly to find her true happiness, and can clearly see a shift in consciousness that has taken place that is empowering her to soar beyond the struggles.

~ **Emmanuel Dagher**, Transformation Healing and Conscious Energy Guide
Los Angeles, CA
www.emmanueldagher.com

—ᴍ—

I'm very thankful to Kimberly for sharing her poems and letting me take part in her life. I'm so touched, and while reading the poems...tears running down my face. I feel with her.... Her fear, her anger...and the feeling of hopelessness. But then she is a warrior and doesn't give up the battle easily. She has taken her path and healed herself. It's nothing to add that Kimberly's poems and experiences expressing herself show her spirit and soul are alive ,pure and bright...it's shining and inspiring to others who also suffered to do the same.... She is absolutely a Healer. I'm blessed to know her and can say proudly... Kim ..she is my friend.

~ **Dr. Hananto Gumuljo**
Deggendorf, Germany

—ᴍ—

I have read Kimberly's poetry a few times over the last month. I love that the work is giving voice to the inner scream for help, her enduring quest for the answers that will make sense of the suffering and bring the healing that she deserves.

> *I cry out to the silence,*
> *'Whatever am I to do?'*
> *"Be gentle with yourself," Spirit replies*
> *"And let My love move through you."*

Ms. Klein's work is both challenging and moving as she brings us deep into the reality of living with a debilitating disease and her powerful urge to heal herself from the inside out.

~ **Antoinette O'Connell**, Homeopathic Healer and Founder of Dragon Light Essences
São Paulo, Brazil
www.dragonenergycenter.com

—⚏—

"Keep on keeping on"

Made in the USA
Lexington, KY
09 October 2016